SOUTH

To my mum Zdeňka and dad Josef for their love and endless support in everything I've attempted.

SOUTH

PHOTOGRAPHS FROM THE
SOUTH ISLAND OF NEW ZEALAND

PETR HLAVACEK

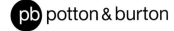 potton & burton

'I regard it as an enormous privilege to be able to live in and photograph the South Island of New Zealand. More than ever, we need to be reminded and inspired to look after these precious wild landscapes, and I only hope my photographs can help to do this.'

Petr Hlavacek
www.nzicescapes.com

Gouland Downs Hut, Heaphy Track, Kahurangi National Park

PREVIOUS PAGES Scott's Beach, Heaphy Track, Kahurangi National Park

Heaphy River, Heaphy Track, Kahurangi National Park

Oparara River, Kahurangi National Park

Moria Gate limestone arch, Oparara Valley, Kahurangi National Park

Wild coastline north of Punakaiki, West Coast

Oparara River, Kahurangi National Park
<small>OVERLEAF</small> Pancake Rocks, Punakaiki, Paparoa National Park

Coastal pools at sunset, near Punakaiki, West Coast

Coastal rocks at sunset, near Punakaiki, West Coast

Blowholes in the Pancake Rocks, Punakaiki, Paparoa National Park

Surge pools between the Pancake Rocks, Punakaiki, Paparoa National Park
OVERLEAF The Southern Alps, framed by kahikatea trees, Fox Glacier, West Coast

Nikau forest, Kohaihai, Kahurangi National Park

A rowi, or Okarito brown kiwi, Westland/Tai Poutini National Park
OVERLEAF Lake Matheson at sunrise, Westland/Tai Poutini National Park

Lichen and moss-covered rocks below the Franz Josef Glacier, Westland/Tai Poutini National Park

Fresh snow on the Franz Josef Glacier, Westland/Tai Poutini National Park
OVERLEAF Aerial view of the névé of the Fox Glacier, Westland/Tai Poutini National Park 27

A helicopter flying above seracs, Franz Josef Glacier, Westland/Tai Poutini National Park

Massive seracs at the head of the Fox Glacier, with Mt Tasman and Aoraki/Mt Cook behind,
Westland/Tai Poutini National Park

A guided party on the Franz Josef Glacier, Westland/Tai Poutini National Park

An ice cave on the lower reaches of the Franz Josef Glacier, Westland/Tai Poutini National Park
OVERLEAF The Southern Alps, seen from Five Mile Lagoon, Westland/Tai Poutini National Park

Sunset lighting up dust on the ice at the head of the Fox Glacier, with Mt Tasman behind,
Westland/Tai Poutini National Park

Sunset over massive seracs at the head of the Fox Glacier, Westland/Tai Poutini National Park
OVERLEAF Sunset on the Southern Alps, from Okarito Trig, Westland/Tai Poutini National Park

The terminus of the Franz Josef Glacier in 2005, Westland/Tai Poutini National Park

The Waiho River flowing out from the terminus of the Franz Josef Glacier,
Westland/Tai Poutini National Park

Ice formations on the Franz Josef Glacier, Westland/Tai Poutini National Park

Ice formations on the Franz Josef Glacier, Westland/Tai Poutini National Park
OVERLEAF Crevasses on the Franz Josef Glacier, Westland/Tai Poutini National Park

Sunrise on farmland near Whataroa, South Westland

Early morning on Alex Knob, with the Fox Glacier behind, Westland/Tai Poutini National Park

Crown ferns, tree ferns and rainforest, Copland Valley, Westland/Tai Poutini National Park

A track through rainforest near Robert Point, Franz Josef, Westland/Tai Poutini National Park
<small>OVERLEAF</small> Evening at Gillespies Beach, Westland/Tai Poutini National Park

A tramper crossing a swingbridge in the Copland Valley, Westland/Tai Poutini National Park

A tramper braves the glacial water of the Copland River, Westland/Tai Poutini National Park

Hot springs at Welcome Flat, Copland Valley, Westland/Tai Poutini National Park

Douglas Rock Hut, upper Copland Valley, Westland/Tai Poutini National Park
OVERLEAF The glacier-fed Copland River, Westland/Tai Poutini National Park

Sunset on Mt Tasman and Aoraki/Mt Cook (right), Westland/Tai Poutini National Park

The beach at Bruce Bay, South Westland

Sunset on the coast south of Okarito, Westland/Tai Poutini National Park

Fishing boats on their moorings, Jackson Bay, South Westland

Road bridge over State Highway 6, looking up toward the Fox Glacier, South Westland

Roaring Billy waterfall, Haast Pass, South Westland

The small terminal lake at the foot of the Brewster Glacier, Mount Aspiring National Park

A tramper descending from Brewster Hut, Mount Aspiring National Park
OVERLEAF Evening light over Lake Wanaka, Central Otago

Glendhu Bay and Lake Wanaka, with Mt Aspiring/Tititea in the distance, Otago

Evening over Lake Hawea, Central Otago

Lake Moke near Queenstown, Central Otago

Evening light over Lake Wanaka, Central Otago

Queenstown and Lake Wakatipu, with The Remarkables behind, Central Otago

The historic TSS *Earnslaw*, Lake Wakatipu, Queenstown, Central Otago

A house in Queenstown, with The Remarkables behind, Central Otago

The Queenstown Gardens, Queenstown, Central Otago

Historic goldfield site on the Kawarau River, Central Otago

The main street of Arrowtown, Central Otago
<small>OVERLEAF</small> Tussock-covered peaks near Wanaka, Central Otago

77

Above the Wakatipu Basin near Arrowtown, with The Remarkables behind, Central Otago

The Arrow River in autumn, near Arrowtown, Central Otago

The Route Burn, flowing alongside the Routeburn Track, Mount Aspiring National Park

The Earland Falls, Routeburn Track, Fiordland National Park

Approaching Harris Saddle on the Routeburn Track, with the Darran Mountains behind, Mount Aspiring National Park

Looking down on the Routeburn Flats, Routeburn Track, Mount Aspiring National Park

Lake Mackenzie, Routeburn Track, Fiordland National Park

Lake Mackenzie, Routeburn Track, Fiordland National Park

The Hollyford Valley, with the Humboldt Mountains behind, Fiordland National Park

Beech forest on the Routeburn Track, Fiordland National Park

Looking down the Cleddau Valley to Milford Sound, Darran Mountains, Fiordland National Park

Walking up towards Barrier Knob, Darran Mountains, Fiordland National Park

Mitre Peak and Milford Sound framed by beech trees, Fiordland National Park

Milford Sound, with Mitre Peak in the distance, Fiordland National Park
OVERLEAF Sunset over the Darran Mountains and Milford Sound, Fiordland National Park

The Hope Arm of Lake Manapouri, Fiordland National Park

Evening on the shores of Lake Manapouri, Fiordland National Park

The Lindis Pass, between the Mackenzie Country and Central Otago

Lake Pukaki, with Aoraki/Mt Cook in the distance, Mackenzie Country
OVERLEAF Lake Pukaki, with Aoraki/Mt Cook in the distance, Mackenzie Country

The terminal lake of the Tasman Glacier, Aoraki/Mount Cook National Park

An iceberg on the terminal lake of the Hooker Glacier, Aoraki/Mount Cook National Park
OVERLEAF Hooker Valley, with Aoraki/Mt Cook behind, Aoraki/Mount Cook National Park   103

Winter sunrise on Mt Sefton and the terminal lake of the Mueller Glacier,
Aoraki/Mount Cook National Park

Swingbridge over the Hooker River, Hooker Valley, Aoraki/Mount Cook National Park
OVERLEAF Winter over the mountains of Aoraki/Mount Cook National Park

107

Road above Akaroa Harbour, Banks Peninsula

Looking down Akaroa Harbour from above Duvauchelle, Banks Peninsula

Timutimu Head at the mouth of Akaroa Harbour, Banks Peninsula

Sunset on the road to the Akaroa Lighthouse, Banks Peninsula
OVERLEAF Winter at Lake Pearson, Waimakariri Basin, Canterbury high country

Sheep grazing at Castle Hill, Waimakariri Basin, Canterbury high country

Winter scene near Porters Pass, with the Craigieburn Range in the distance,
Canterbury high country

Looking up the Waimakariri River, Arthur's Pass National Park

The Otira Viaduct, near Arthur's Pass, Arthur's Pass National Park
OVERLEAF The outer reaches of Pelorus Sound, seen from Mt Stokes, Marlborough Sounds

Governors Bay, Grove Arm, Queen Charlotte Sound, Marlborough Sounds

Long Island, seen from Motuara Island, outer Queen Charlotte Sound, Marlborough Sounds
OVERLEAF Keneperu Sound, part of Pelorus Sound, Marlborough Sounds

A vineyard in the Wairau Valley near Blenheim, Marlborough

Lake Rotoiti with the St Arnaud Range behind, Nelson Lakes National Park

Evening light near Rocks Hut, with Mt Richmond in the distance, Mount Richmond Forest Park

The Pelorus River, Mount Richmond Forest Park

Golden sands at Totaranui, Abel Tasman National Park

Watering Cove, Abel Tasman National Park

Low tide at Stilwell Bay, Abel Tasman National Park